Let's go camping

Written by Heather Haylock
Illustrated by Mauro Mazzara

a Capstone company — publishers for children

I'm Oliver.

In the spring I go camping with my grandad. Have you ever been camping? You can come with us. I will tell you what we like to do.

What do we need?
Grandad will bring the tent, chairs and camp beds. He will pack the food and drinks.

Here is what I will pack in my backpack.

- ✓ sleeping bag
- ✓ fishing net
- ✓ torch
- ✓ strong boots
- ✓ jacket
- ✓ sunhat
- ✓ sunscreen
- ✓ book

But I will not pack this!

Let's go!

Grandad comes to pick me up in his old van. He took my dad camping in this van when Dad was little. It is an old, old van. It starts with a bit of a growl and then we are off.

Grandad and I chat for a bit. Then I check the map to see how far there is to go. We are not near to the camp yet. It is a long trip, so I drop off to sleep.

Can you see the start and end of our trip?

Setting up camp

"Here we are," says Grandad. "Let's get a good spot for the tent."
We look for a flat spot with no lumps, bumps or rocks.
We must not put the tent up right by the creek. When it rains, the creek comes up high and the tent might float off. That's not good. We look for a spot with no trees. A tree must not crash down on the tent!

Can you see a good spot for our tent?

Grandad and I put up the tent. I peg it down so the wind cannot lift it up. It is hard to push the tent pegs into the soil, so I bang them in with a hammer.

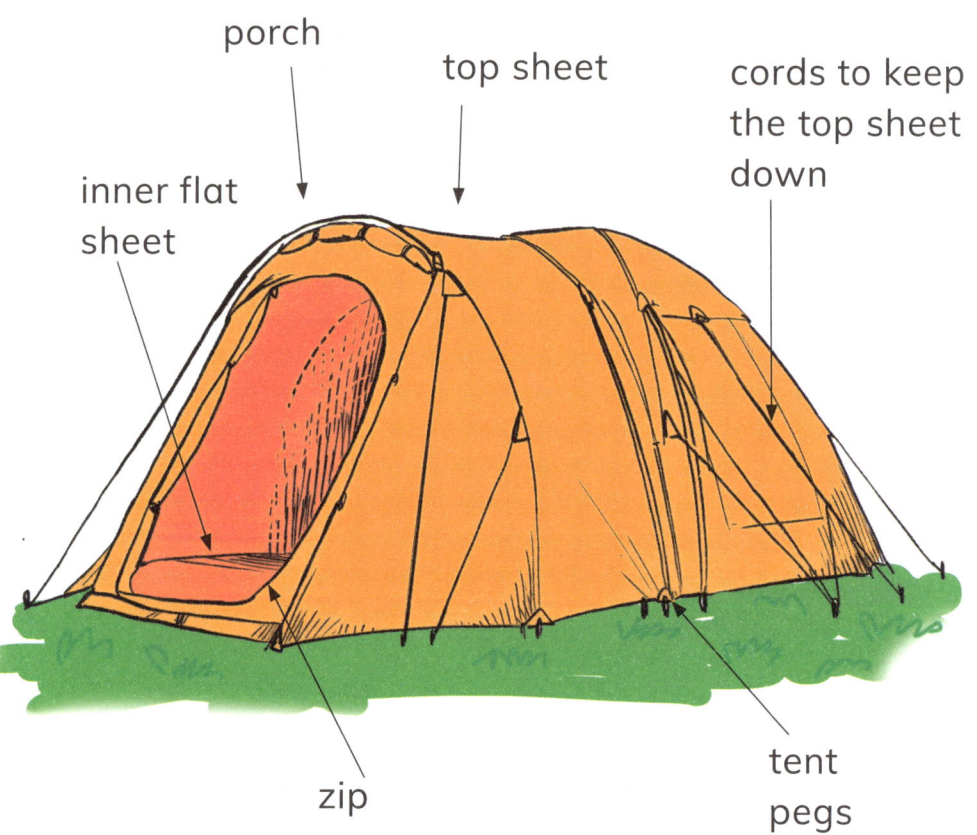

Grandad sorts out our stuff. The camp beds go in the tent with our sleeping bags on top.

We put our backpacks in the tent too, so that if it rains they will not get wet. Now that we are set up, the camping fun can start!

Getting dinner

"No fish, no dinner!" says Grandad. He is the cook when we are camping.
We go down to the river with our net. I get a fish, but it is too little so I toss it back in the river. We wait and wait. No fish!
"No dinner for us tonight, Oliver!" Grandad tells me with a wink.

Camp cook-up

Back at camp, Grandad grins. We are in luck – he has a tub full of lots of food to cook! We do not need the fish, thank goodness!

And he has a tub full of choc-chip muffins, too! We keep the lid on tight to stop ants getting them.

Up to the stars

When night comes, we go up the hill next to the camp. We sit in the darkness at the top. All is still. We look up.

It is not so dark up there. There are lots and lots of stars. Big stars and little stars, blinking at us.

Then I hear, "Woo? Woo?"
I jump a little.
"What is that?"
"It's just owls in the trees," Grandad says. "They go hunting for food at night."

Looking for eels

"Let's go and look for eels," says Grandad. "Eels hunt at night, too."
So we go back down the hill. Soon I can hear the creek, but it is too dark to see much. I turn my torch on and look under weeds and rocks.
Grandad stoops to look.
Then I spot one. "Look! A long, dark eel!"
"I see it," says Grandad. "It is hunting for little fish and snails."

Off to bed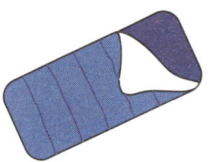

We brush our teeth and get into the tent.
I zip it shut to keep the bugs out. Then I turn my torch on and get my book out.
I can hear the owls.
I can hear the creek.
I flick my torch off.
We zip our sleeping bags up tight.
"Good night, sleep tight," says Grandad.

Wet, wet, wet

It is morning. I hear drips! I unzip the tent and look out. It's raining!
"What will we do today?" Grandad says. Rain is no problem for us. We like the rain as much as the sun when we are camping. We still have fun, as long as we bring the right gear.
"Let's go trekking," I tell him.

A trek in the wet

We put on our boots and jackets. Then we set out on a long trek in the rain. Our boots stop our feet getting wet. We stand by the creek. It is getting higher.

"Let's go back to the tent now," says Grandad. "I am getting a chill."

We put up a string to hang our wet things on. I put up the tent's porch so we can sit in our chairs without getting soaked. Grandad boils up hot drinks for us. We chat as we sip our drinks and look at the rain. There will be no stars out tonight.

Fun in the sun

"I cannot hear drips today, Oliver,"
says Grandad, in the morning.
I unzip the tent. The rain has stopped.
"The sun is out," I tell him.
"What shall we do?" he says.
"Let's go swimming!" I yell.
"Good plan!" he grins.

We do not need our boots today. The rocks feel hot under our feet as we go down to the creek.
I float on my back. Grandad sits on a rock and soaks his feet. I splash him a little bit. Then he splashes me a lot.

I float to the far bank. I dig my fingers into the rocks and a lizard runs out. I did not expect that!

Packing up

We are going today. Grandad sweeps the dust from the tent. I pull out the tent pegs and check the tent is not wet. If we pack it wet, it will rot and be no good for camping next year.
We pick up rubbish. We like our camping spot to look better when we go than it did when we got there.
We will come camping here for years and years.